# Festivals

# My Baisakhi

D1407334

Little Nippers

**www.heinemann.co.uk/library**
Visit our website to find out more information about **Heinemann Library** books.

To order:
☎ Phone 44 (0) 1865 888066
▤ Send a fax to 44 (0) 1865 314091
▭ Visit the Heinemann Bookshop at www.heinemann.co.uk/library to browse our catalogue and order online.

First published in Great Britain by Heinemann Library, Halley Court, Jordan Hill, Oxford OX2 8EJ, part of Harcourt Education. Heinemann is a registered trademark of Harcourt Education Ltd.

Editorial: Sarah Eason and Louise Galpine
Design: Jo Hinton-Malivoire and Tokay, Bicester, UK (www.tokay.co.uk)
Picture Research: Ruth Blair
Production: Severine Ribierre

Originated by Dot Gradations Ltd
Printed and bound in China by South China Printing Company

ISBN 0 431 16262 X (hardback)
09 08 07 06 05
10 9 8 7 6 5 4 3 2 1

ISBN 0 431 16266 2 (paperback)
09 08 07 06 05
10 9 8 7 6 5 4 3 2 1

**British Library Cataloguing in Publication Data**
Hughes, Monica
Little Nippers Festivals My Baisakhi
394.2'6546
A full catalogue record for this book is available from the British Library.

**Acknowledgements**
The Publishers would like to thank the following for permission to reproduce photographs:
Art Directors/TRIP pp. **12**, **13**, **14** (Beryl Dhanjal); Corbis/RF p. **22**; World Religions Photo Library pp. **10**, **11**, **20–21**; all other pictures Harcourt Education/Tudor Photography.

Cover photograph inside the Gurdwara, reproduced with permission of Harcourt Education/Tudor Photography.

The Publishers would like to thank Philip Emmett for his assistance in the preparation of this book.

Every effort has been made to contact copyright holders of any material reproduced in this book. Any omissions will be rectified in subsequent printings if notice is given to the Publishers.

# Contents

I like telling my friends and my teacher about being a Sikh.

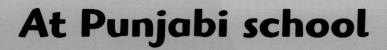

I've been practising for the poetry competition. I'm almost ready now.

I'm writing a card for my cousins in India.

Don't I look **smart** in my new Baisakhi clothes?

9

# Outside the Gurdwara

Baisakhi is a special time at our Gurdwara.

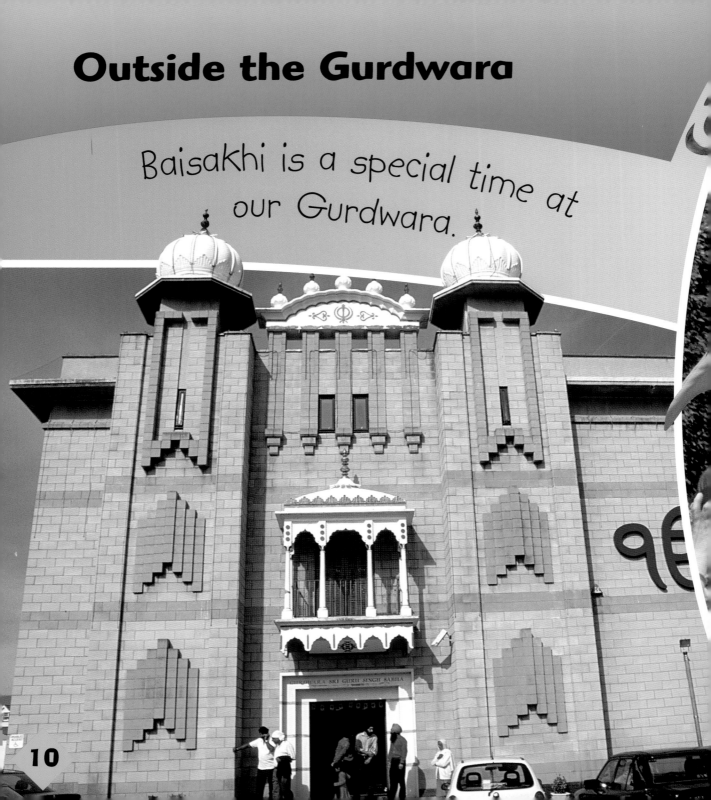

The flagpole is taken down so that we can put up the new flag.

# The Baisakhi procession

Here come the Five Beloved.
They lead the procession.

**Look!**
Here come the
Gatka dancers.

# Happy Baisakhi!

Look at that **fantastic** float.

I'm really excited!

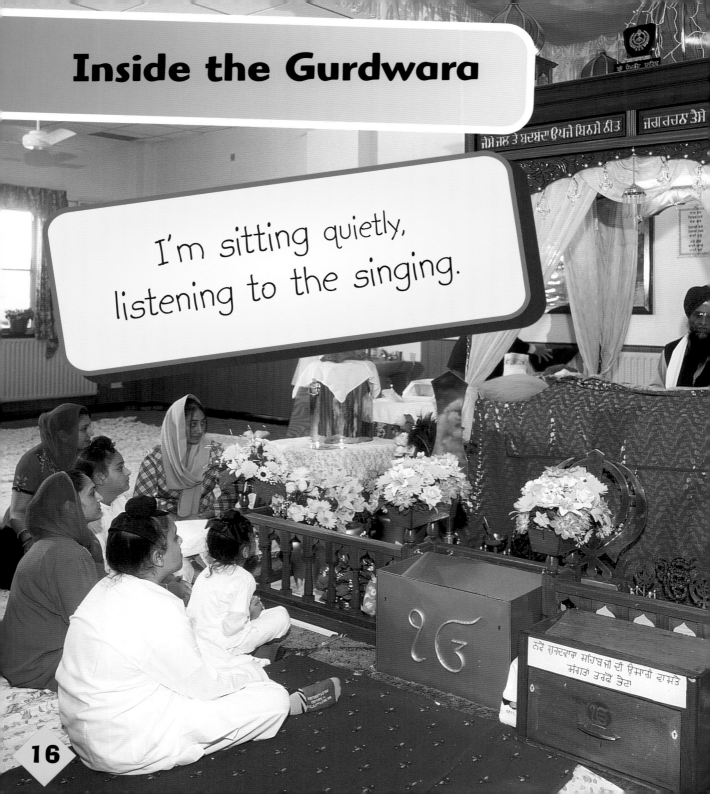

# Inside the Gurdwara

I'm sitting quietly, listening to the singing.

We hear readings from the Guru Granth Sahib.

Thank you!

I'm having a helping of karah parshad.

# Let's celebrate!

Look at the Bhangra dancers.
They are really good.

# The day ends

I love the fair. There are lots of **rides** to go on – and lots to eat!

It has been a **wonderful** Baisakhi.

# Index

The end

## Notes for adults

Most festivals and celebrations share common elements that will be familiar to the young child, such as new clothes, special food, sending and receiving cards and presents, giving to charity, being with family and friends and a busy and exciting build-up time. It is important that the child has an opportunity to compare and contrast their own experiences with those of the children in the book.

The following Early Learning Goals are relevant to this series:

*Knowledge and understanding of the world*
- Early learning goals for exploration and investigation: Discuss events that occur regularly within the children's experience, for example seasonal patterns, daily routines, celebrations

*Personal, social and emotional development*
- Early learning goals for a sense of community
- Respond to significant experiences, showing a range of feelings when appropriate
- Have a developing respect for their own cultures and beliefs and those of other people

Baisakhi celebrates the start of the Sikh New Year and is held in mid-April. It lasts for three days and during this time the Guru Granth Sahib, the Sikh Holy Book, is read from beginning to end at the Gurdwara. The flag flying outside the Gurdwara is taken down with much ceremony. The flagpole is cleaned and a new flag raised. There are lively processions in the streets leading to the Gurdwara. After prayers, hymns and readings everyone gathers for a communal meal in the Langar – the dining room in the Gurdwara. There are often fairs and dancing in the evening.